PUEBLO GIRLS

PUEBLO GIRLS
Growing Up in Two Worlds

MARCIA KEEGAN

Clear Light Publishers
Santa Fe, New Mexico

Sonja and Desiree's Dedication

To Our Parents,
Renee and Leon Roybal

Copyright © 1999 Marcia Keegan

Clear Light Publishers, 823 Don Diego, Santa Fe, New Mexico 87501
WEB: www.clearlightbooks.com

First Edition
10 9 8 7 6 5 4 3 2 1

Keegan, Marcia.
     Pueblo girls : growing up in two worlds / by Marcia Keegan.
                    p. cm.
     Summary: Text and photographs depict the home, school, and cultural life of two young Indian girls growing up on the San Ildefonso Pueblo in New Mexico.
     ISBN 1-57416-020-6
     1. Roybal, Sonja. 2. Roybal, Desiree. 3. Tewa girls—New Mexico—San Ildefonso—Juvenile literature. 4. Tewa women potters—New Mexico—San Ildefonso—Juvenile literature. 5. Tewa Indians—Social life and customs—Juvenile literature. 6. San Ildefonso (N.M.)—Social life and customs—Juvenile literature. [1. Roybal, Sonja. 2. Roybal, Desiree. 3. Pueblo Indians—Biography. 4. Pueblo Indians—Social life and customs. 5. Indians of North America—New Mexico—Biography. 6. Indians of North America—New Mexico—Social life and customs.]
I. Title
e99.T35K44 1998   98-30831
978.9'56—dc21   CIP
                                                                        AC

Printed in Hong Kong
Design by Marcia Keegan
Production and typography by Carol O'Shea

Sonja Roybal is a ten-year-old Pueblo Indian girl, and her sister Desiree is eight years old. These sisters, besides doing the things any other girls would do, follow the traditions of their Native American heritage.

Sonja's Indian name is *Tunn-Povi*, which means Basket Flower. Desiree's Indian name is *Pohn-muu-whá*, which means Early Morning Dew. When Pueblo children are born, they receive their Indian names first.

When the Spanish explorers first came to New Mexico and Arizona in the 1500s, they found the Native Americans living in villages. The Spanish called these villages *pueblos*, meaning "small towns." It is from this that the Pueblo Indians took their name.

Sonja and Desiree live at San Ildefonso Pueblo, which is twenty-two miles north of Santa Fe, New Mexico, on the east bank of the river known as the Rio Grande. Their Pueblo lies between the massive peaks of the Jemez and Sangre de Cristo mountains. The six hundred Indians of the Pueblo live in one-story houses built of the sun-baked mud and straw mixture called *adobe*.

The village looks much the same as it has for hundreds of years, and the houses look and feel like part of the earth. Sonja and Desiree's modern house is made from the same adobe material as their ancestors' homes.

Desiree and Sonja go hiking and have picnics with their parents, Leon and Renee, near Black Mesa, which is behind their house.

San Ildefonso Indians believe Black Mesa is the home of their ancestral spirits. The people of San Ildefonso believe that spirits live in the earth, the sky, the waters, and in special sacred places.

The Pueblo Indians believe that Chavayo, the protector spirit, lives in Black Mesa. Chavayo protects the children from harm, but also visits them when they misbehave.

The girls ride the bus to school in nearby Pojoaque. Sonja goes to the intermediate school and Desiree goes to the elementary school. The elementary school has classes from kindergarten through the fourth grade, and the intermediate school serves grades five and six.

Tewa is the native language of the San Ildefonso people. It is one of the five languages spoken by the Pueblo Indians dating back to prehistoric times.

Sonja and Desiree do much of their school work on computers, both at school and at home.

They also like to play games and send e-mail letters to their cousin Tim Roybal. He is a sophomore at Denver University.

After school, Sonja and Desiree play. Sonja plays basketball, and Desiree rides her bike and plays with dolls. The girls also play video games at the mall. At home, they play Nintendo. Their favorite game is Super Mario Kart. Sonja says, "Desiree gets mad 'cause she always loses. So I try not to win all the time." Desiree says, "But she always wins."

Like most girls their age, Sonja and Desiree have homework. They do their assignments together in the living room of their home. To help with their studies, the girls have a home computer. In these ways, their lives are as modern as those of any other girls.

Desiree has lots of Barbie dolls and stuffed toys. She likes to play dolls with her neighbor Colleen. The girls like to make up weddings and parties. They play the "Wedding March" on their electronic keyboard.

Both Sonja and Desiree like school. Desiree says, "I like PE, music, and computer classes, and I like to draw. I like to swing and play on the monkey bars." She also likes phonics and reading.

Sonja says, "I like recess." Then she adds, "I like computer, language, and spelling classes."

Sonja and Desiree practice cheerleading with their cousins. Desiree stands on top, held up by Sonja and cousin Francine. Darrylinn cheers in front.

Sonja does her homework and looks for Tibet on her new globe. She is writing a paper called "Free Tibet." Tibet is a country in Asia that has been occupied by China since 1959. The Dalai Lama is the spiritual and political leader of Tibet and now lives in India. Sonja and Desiree met the Dalai Lama when he came to visit New Mexico. After meeting the Dalai Lama, Sonja said, "When I grow up, I want to help the Tibetans get their freedom and their country back."

Sonja's pet dog Shadow is four years old. Shadow likes to play ball with Sonja. Sonja is in charge of feeding Shadow and has taken special care of her since she hurt her foot. Sonja says, "She's a very good watchdog at night. She always greets me when I come home from school." She runs ahead of the car when the girls go to their grandmother's. Sonja says Shadow got her name because she is afraid of her own shadow.

Sonja loves to play basketball and is on the school team, called the "Fawnettes." They play other school teams in nearby Santa Fe and Española.

Desiree is a cheerleader at school, and her six-year-old cousin Evan is on the football team.

Desiree and Sonja's mother, Renee, shows them how to make pottery using coils of clay. San Ildefonso is world famous for the beautiful black pottery made by the women of the Pueblo. Sonja and Desiree's great-great-grandmother was the famous potter, Maria Martinez.

The girls' mother makes distinctive Pueblo pottery in the traditional way. She makes micaceous pottery from glittery brown clay. She rolls coils of clay and puts them on top of each other, then shapes the pot gently. Next it will be dried, sanded, polished, and finally fired outdoors.

On weekdays Renee works as a computer technician at Los Alamos Laboratory.

Grandfather Julian Martinez shows the girls how to make headdresses for a dance. Their grandfather makes headdresses with feathers from red tail hawks, spotted tail hawks, and eagle tails. He is a drummer, dancer, and lead singer at the Pueblo.

Grandfather Julian sings the girls a song in Tewa. In English it goes something like this:

"When the Hawk flies over your head,
Or the Eagle's shadow falls across you on the trail,
Under those silent wings you are guarded;
Golden eyes watch over you
And protect you on the path."

The Pueblo Indians consider the sun, earth, moon, stars, wind, water, lightning, thunder, and all living things sacred. The people sing and dance to make rain fall, make crops grow, give thanks for the health of crops and people, and cure illness.

Every Pueblo Indian is a member of a clan, such as the Parrot Clan, Sun Clan, Spider Clan, Corn Clan, or Fire Clan. There are over 100 clans. Children from San Ildefonso become members of their father's clan. Sonja and Desiree were born into the Corn Clan. Each clan is responsible for different ceremonies and dances that the Pueblo Indians believe help maintain the balance of nature.

Pueblo Indians plant a special type of corn that has very long roots and grows well in New Mexico, where there is very little rain. Indian corn grows in several colors: yellow, blue, red, and white.

Traditionally, corn is the foundation of Pueblo Indian life. Without corn, Pueblo ways could not have survived. In the past, corn made up a large part of the Indian diet, and it has always been regarded with deep respect and reverence. Hardly a ceremony exists that does not use corn or cornmeal in some way. Since corn and other crops can't grow without water, Pueblo people perform their rain dances, prayers, and other practices as a regular part of ceremonial life.

Sonja and Desiree's father Leon shows the girls an ancient drawing of a sundial in a secluded area on the Pueblo lands. Their father explains that the drawing, called a *petroglyph*, was used as a calendar by their ancient ancestors nearly a thousand years ago.

Leon works at the Pueblo of San Ildefonso as the natural resource director. He oversees all the lands of the San Ildefonso Pueblo.

Sonja and Desiree help their grandmother, Mary Martinez, bake bread. The women of the village bake bread in outdoor ovens called *hornos*, just as their ancestors did. After the wood fire inside burns out, the ashes are removed, and the dough is placed in the oven to bake. The adobe oven stays hot enough to bake the bread even though there is no fire.

Feast days are special times with day-long dances and lots of good food. After dancing, the family comes to Grandmother Julia's house. She serves them bread she has made in the horno and offers many other feast-day foods such as stews, pinto beans, bread pudding, corn, and fruit pies. Grandmother Julia is famous for her red chile stew.

Sonja and Desiree like to visit Bandelier National Monument, where their ancestors once lived. This long-abandoned Indian village is ten miles from their home. Sonja and Desiree wonder what it was like when their people used to live there. Sonja says, "It's kind of weird how they lived then, with no electricity." No one has lived there since the 1500s, but many people come from all over the world to visit Bandelier today.

Sonja and Desiree's ancestors climbed ladders to get to caves carved in the cliffs. The girls have fun climbing up and down the ladders and the cliffs.

Sonja hangs out with her cousins, Darrylinn, Francine, and Darlene. Desiree sits in the doorway of an ancient house at Bandelier.

The cousins climb ladders and play inside the caves.

From left to right: Darlene, Francine, Desiree, Sonja, and Darrylinn.

The family goes fishing at the Rio Grande behind their house. The Pueblos were established along the Rio Grande.

Once every summer their grandfather takes the girls on a special all-day fishing trip. They enjoy this fishing trip very much. "Grandma Mary packs a delicious picnic lunch," Desiree says. "She packs every little detail." Sonja has caught four fish and Desiree has caught two. Desiree says she is a little afraid to touch the fish. She thinks they are slimy and they jump around too much. Sonja says that Desiree is afraid the fish will bite her.

Both Desiree and her mother like to eat fish tails, because they are crunchy. Sonja thinks that is gross.

Grandfather Julian helps Desiree catch a rainbow trout while Sonja looks on.

Desiree receives her First Holy Communion from Father Wayne. She says she felt happy at her Communion. She had to memorize many prayers.

The Pueblo Indians follow their own religious traditions as well as those of the Catholic Church. The original San Ildefonso Church was built in the 1600s and rebuilt in 1964 on the same site.

After her Communion, Desiree plays with her cat, Milo, who she says likes to stretch, eat, lie around, and roll in sand. Sometimes Desiree dresses her in doll clothes. Milo doesn't like that. Milo likes Sonja's dog Shadow. They eat together, and they curl up together and sleep.

There are nineteen Pueblos in New Mexico, and the Pueblo people speak five different languages. Sonja and Desiree speak Tewa, their native language, as well as English. Many Pueblo Indians also speak Spanish. Ancient songs are in Tewa, and the girls have been dancing in the traditional ceremonies since they were two years old.

All Pueblos have a special room known as the *kiva*. It is different from ordinary living areas. Kivas are large rooms, often circular, where religious ceremonies take place. The dancers go to the kiva to prepare for the dances. Public parts of the ceremonies are held in the plazas, but the private portions are held in the kiva. Sonja and Desiree's village kiva is in the middle of the central plaza, right across from the church.

Sonja's mother helps her dress for a dance. The rituals, beliefs, and prayers of the Pueblo Indians are spoken and sung but not written down. Desiree and Sonja are learning these traditions from their parents. The girls will teach what they are learning to their own children.

The Pueblo Indian spiritual life is based on a yearly cycle tied to the agricultural growing seasons. Corn Dances are held in the spring and fall, while during the winter, animal dances like the Deer and Buffalo Dances are held.

The Indians of San Ildefonso perform the Corn Dance in September in honor of Saint Anthony. They bring the statue of the saint out of the church to watch the dance.

The Corn Dance is a day-long ceremony of thanksgiving. The people thank nature for blessings that help the tribe live in harmony with the earth. The Indians believe that by dancing they preserve the cycle of the seasons and the fruitfulness of the earth.

Grandmother Julia helps Sonja get ready for a dance. The dances are prayers, and people of all ages who live at the Pueblo join in the dance.

The dances are silent prayers. Sonja says, "When I dance the Corn Dance, I get serious. When I start to dance, I think about how my people before me were and how they lived. But mostly I think about my grandfather J.D., who passed on before I was born."

Dances are held several times a year. The men decide the number of dances each year. Children participate in some of the dances. Sonja and Desiree have danced in as many as seven a year.

When the girls are going to be in a dance, they have to practice every night, after their homework. They wear traditional clothes and follow strict rules for the ceremonial dance preparations.

Sonja says, "I like to dance. It gives me energy and makes me feel good. I experience something that doesn't happen every day. I go out of my normal life and experience something real important."

The dancers follow the beat of the drummers and singers. The drumbeat is like the heartbeat of the earth. The prayers and songs are sung to the earth, the sky, the rain, the clouds, the spirits, and the four directions—north, south, east, and west.

Desiree says, "My grandpa sings good and has been singing all his life. When I'm dancing, I can hear my grandpa singing and drumming. I feel happy, because he is there."

The girls' father is Head War Captain of the North Kiva. He has many responsibilities, including guarding the dancers and being the caretaker of the kiva. The girls are proud of their father. Desiree says, "When I dance, I know he is watching everyone, but especially he watches us."

Sonja and Desiree wear feathered headdresses for the Comanche Dance. The dance came to their Pueblo in the early 1800s, when the Comanche Indians came to trade with the Pueblo people. They used to get together to teach each other songs and dances. The Comanche Dance is now done on the San Ildefonso Feast Day, January 23rd.

Sonja and Desiree are proud of their Indian heritage. They learn dances and songs that have been passed from parents to children for 10,000 years. Sonja and Desiree belong to two cultures, the traditional Pueblo Indian world and the twenty-first century world of computers. They feel they have the best of both worlds. When they grow up, they will teach their children the Pueblo Indian ways that preserve the regular passing of the seasons and the fruitfulness of the earth.